Trials and

Life at The Bar

Margaret Barnes
The Scribbling Advocate

The right of Margaret Barnes to be identified as the author of this work has been asserted in accordance with the Copyright, Designs and Patents Act 1988.

Foreword

I spent my working life as an advocate in the Criminal Justice System of England and Wales, first as a solicitor and then as a barrister. These stories are my experiences told without elaboration. I have changed the names to protect both the innocent and the guilty but the events they describe are true.

They took place in a variety of courts up and down the country. I have not attempted to describe them. Some like the Assize Court at Lancaster and the No 1 Court at the Central Criminal Court are huge impressive rooms where the presiding Judge looks down on the barristers, clerks and police officers. Most are more modest.

Finally this small book is dedicated to all those advocates who fight for their client without fear or favour, and in particular to Kate Mallinson who throughout her life did just that.

Going Equipped with Who's Who

The offence of going equipped to commit burglary doesn't seem to feature in the courts these days, but as an articled clerk I was sent to sit behind Mark Carlisle on just such a case. The two defendants, both male, had been apprehended in one of the lanes in the countryside inland from the coastal resort of Blackpool. The evidence against them consisted of observations by the police to whom they were well known, linked with the various objects found inside their car, a grey Vauxhall, I think.

The offence took place on a summer's evening when an observant police officer had seen the two men, Ken and Norman, driving along a narrow lane that led down towards the River Wyre. He knew it was a dead end, so he radioed for help and an unmarked car arrived. When the Vauxhall emerged from the lane and turned along the main road, the police car followed at a discrete distance. The Vauxhall then turned down another of the lanes which went towards the River, another dead end. The police stayed on the main road keeping watch. This was repeated a third time, but this time the police followed and as it reached the entrance to a large house set in extensive grounds, they indicated the Vauxhall was to pull over.

Norman and Ken got out of the car and went to meet the officers. As the two policemen, DC Smith and DC McKie, approached Norman, he pulled his wallet from the back pocket of his trousers and began searching through it.

'Here's my driving licence and I've got insurance as well,' Norman said, waving the pieces of paper under DC Smith's nose.

'Thanks,' said the officer, pushing away Norman's arm. 'Let's have a look in the car shall we.'

All four men strode towards the car. 'What you doing round here?' DC McKie said, rolling his r's. He made direct eye contact with Ken, who dropped his gaze.

'Looking for work. Been told some guy wanted a job on his roof,' Ken said.

'What's this guy's name then?' McKie said.

'Don't know, just told where he lived.'

By this time they had all reached the vehicle and the two officers opened the boot. Inside was a bag of tools, spanners, screw drivers, a couple of hammers, and laid across the base the dark metal of a crowbar glinted in the low summer sun.

'Doing a roof were we, with a crowbar?' McKie wasn't expecting an answer.

Norman spluttered. 'Yes, guv. We were going to see this guy about some work.'

'Where does he live, this bloke you were going to see?' Smith said, as he opened the front passenger door.

On the floor was a piece of paper torn from a reporter's notepad, the type anyone can buy in WH Smith's. 'We had a map...' Ken pushed past the officer, leant into the vehicle and picked up the sheet of paper. 'We'd met this guy in the pub. Said he had a few jobs we could do and he drew this map of where his house was. Here, see.' He thrust the piece of paper into DC Smith's hand.

The map had been drawn by an inexpert hand, but it clearly showed a lane off the main Cleveleys to Singleton Road. The drawing showed two or three houses along a twisting lane that led down towards the River.

DC Smith sucked his teeth as he contemplated whether to arrest the two men. He didn't believe a word they were saying, but with a good defence lawyer they would probably be acquitted. Was it worth the paperwork involved; whatever they were up to they had been stopped in their tracks.

'Well not sure...' the officer said, but was interrupted by DC McKie who was holding a book in his hand.

'What's this? A copy of *Who's Who*. Now what would you be wanting with this then?'

They were arrested and charged with going equipped with a crow bar, spanners, various tools and a copy of *Who's Who*. Despite Mr Carlisle best endeavours both men were convicted.

Oysters with George

I suppose George Carman was one of the more colourful members of the Bar and my first meeting with him confirmed that view. I was still an articled clerk - one may have been a trainee solicitor, but the term general dogsbody seemed more appropriate. One of the many jobs I was given was to attend with counsel in the courts where more serious offences were tried. On this occasion I was sent to Blackpool Quarter Sessions to sit behind George during a case of causing death by dangerous driving.

He was a small rather busy man, always dressed in pinstripe trousers with a black jacket and the silk waistcoat worn by QC's. The client was pleading guilty to the charge and after a rather tedious conference with him, George went off to do some work in the robing room. I was left sitting with the client until, about half an hour before the mid day adjournment, I was summoned to see George.

'Go and find out if there is any chance of our case coming on before lunch,' he said. I did as I was told and scurried off to find the court usher. My enquiries revealed that we were unlikely to be called before the court rose. I returned with the news to the robing room. When I told George he snorted and said, 'Damn, well I suppose we'd better make the best of it. Do you know where Robert's Oyster Shop is on the promenade?'

It was a silly question; everyone living in Blackpool knew where to get oysters. I told him I did. 'Good. Go and tell Robert I want a dozen oysters and a pint of Guiness and tell him I'll pop in and pay later.'

I was to meet George on many occasions; there were a few other cases while I was still an articled clerk and then when I was living in London and had become a barrister, we frequented the same drinking holes, but I was never in the same case as him again until a few years later on in my career. That was in early 1981 when I was instructed to represent a solicitor who was charged with defrauding the Legal Aid Fund of many thousands of pounds. The case was tried in Manchester and I was being led by the leader of the Northern Circuit Mick Mcguire and George was prosecuting. As George called the witnesses, court clerks and law society staff we began to undermine the prosecution case. It was based upon a number of false premises, one of which was that a bail application would only take ten minutes of court time. That was torpedoed when a bail application was interposed in our trial; the High Court Judge said it would only take fifteen minutes at the most. It took over an hour as Mick Mcguire pointed out, much to the Judge's annoyance.

George was clearly getting rattled as we exposed the weaknesses in the prosecution again and again. Eventually one lunch time we heard him on the telephone to the Director of Public Prosecutions. 'I can take a few bullet holes below the waterline but a bombshell is too much.'

No oysters for George that day.

A sack of potatoes and a bottle of Teepol.

Not a murder, but still one of the most interesting cases I was involved in. The client, Max was a fisherman. He sailed in small boats out of Fleetwood, when there was still a fishing fleet in that north Lancashire town. The basis that these small trawlers worked on was called share fishing. The boat's owners took the major share of the profits on the catch and the remainder was split between the crew. On this trip the *Goodwill* had a crew of five. Max was the fishing skipper; the defacto captain of the ship. He wasn't a certificated captain so an older man was the official skipper, but Max really ran the boat and directed where they would sail and where they would put the nets down. He was the man with the 'nose' for the shoals.

This particular night they were fishing in the Irish Sea. One of the crew was on watch and Max had gone to his bunk to sleep. The sea was running high and the small boat rolled and pitched. It was cold and the fire in the cabin had been lit. Suddenly the boat was hit by a large wave and the gas bottle in the galley, secured in place by a sack of potatoes and a bottle of Teepol, came loose and rolled along the deck and into the cabin.

Max was woken as the gas from the bottle exploded. He grabbed his clothes and ran through a wall of fire onto the deck. The rest of the crew had already got the lifeboat over the side and they all jumped into it. They were in the life raft for three days before they were picked up by another boat and taken to the Isle of Man. Here Max was treated for the burns he had suffered as he dashed from the cabin. He needed extensive skin grafts to his face and hands. Despite being very disfigured, his nose had melted in the heat, he had lost his eyebrows and his lips were misshaped, he was devastatingly charming

He sued the boats owners for damages for the injuries he had sustained, on the basis they had failed to provide proper housing for the gas bottle in the galley. The owners denied liability saying they were not his employers but co-adventurers and did not owe a duty of care to him or the rest of the crew. The judge disagreed and awarded Max substantial damages, but said they would have been much more had Max not been so determined to overcome his injuries.

I had driven then to the final hearing in my principal's car which broke down on the way back. Fortunately my passengers were too elated to worry about the delay caused and waited patiently at the roadside until we were rescued by the AA.

Discretion Statement.

Before the law on Divorce altered in the early 1970's the petitioner – that's the person seeking the divorce - had to establish one of a number of matrimonial offences. Cruelty, adultery, or separation for two years were the main causes. Further because it was what was called an *equitable relief,* the clue is in the word petitioner rather than plaintiff, the husband or wife seeking the divorce had to come to the court *'with clean hands.'* In practice this caused a lot of problems as very often the petitioner was in another relationship and was committing adultery. In order to overcome this difficulty which would have prevented a divorce being granted the courts had established the procedure known as a discretion statement. In effect the erring party asked the court to grant their petition for a divorce not withstanding their own adultery.

Soon after I qualified as a solicitor I had just such a case. The wife, Helen Broad was a glamorous blonde. She had left her husband and was living with another man. She and I discussed at length how to deal with her discretion statement and agreed on a wording that essentially said she had entered into another relationship and had committed adultery on numerous occasions over the preceding two years. The statement was signed by her and placed in a sealed envelope, as was the practice.

On the day of the hearing of Helen Broad's petition, we met David Grimshaw, the barrister I had instructed to appear on her behalf, in the waiting area of the County Court. He towered over both me and the client, as I introduced them.

Helen was wearing a pale camel coat, her long hair was loose and her lips were painted with a bright red lipstick. She was the best looking woman in the room and David took her hand and held onto it for a little longer than necessary, before directing us to a quiet a corner where he could discuss the case and try to put Helen at ease. David manoeuvred his not inconsiderable bulk down onto a chair and pulled it up close to where we were sitting on a bench.

'Is there a discretion statement?' he said.

I searched through my file and handed him the brown envelope containing the carefully crafted disclosure. He opened it, his heavy fingers tearing the paper apart and rather more delicately opened the piece of paper inside. He fished his glasses out of the top pocket of his dark pin-striped suit and began to read. The petitioner watched him, her mouth in a wide smile but the eyes suggested she was a little wary.

David looked over the top of his glasses, 'Don't you know how many times you have committed adultery?'

Helen Broad looked him straight in the face and said, 'I don't count, do you?'

Death of the Mandie Queen

The cell under the court rooms at Blackpool was bare, the walls and floor the dull grey of unpainted concrete. There was no furniture. In the corner of the room crouched down, his head touching his knees, and rocking to and fro was the figure of my client, Malcolm D. He was dressed in a curious mix of ill-fitting clothes garnered from some unknown source; his own clothes having been taken for examination by forensic scientists. The door of the cell closed with the thud of heavy metal behind me and for a moment the rocking ceased as he looked in my direction.

'I loved her. Why would I kill her?'

'Do you want to tell me about it?' I said.

The rocking began again. As I waited I thought about Malcolm's wife, Lynn, a thin anxious woman in her early twenties and known locally as the Mandie Queen, on account of her swallowing Mandrax tablets like they were sweets. Her body had been found three days before lying naked on their bed in a rundown holiday flat on South Shore. The pathologist said she had died as a result of vagal inhibition when pressure was applied to her neck. That assault had resulted in the hyoid bone in her neck being fractured. Furthermore, although her blood contained a high level of the drugs, they had not been the cause of death, indeed the level was insufficient to have killed her.

Malcolm continued to insist he had not murdered her. He said they had both smoked some cannabis and taken other illegally obtained drugs. Lynn had been totally out of it but was demanding he go and get some food. He'd left her and gone to a local shop where he'd bought some bread, ham and milk. When he returned to the flat she was lying on the bed asleep, but when he tried to rouse her he couldn't. He felt for her pulse and then realised she wasn't breathing. There was a stash of drugs in the flat, which he decided to get rid of before calling the police, but then he panicked and decided to run for it.

'I loved her, why would I kill her?' he repeated.

I didn't tell him that I was aware he had been violent towards her in the past. Lynn had been to see me a few weeks previously, asking me to represent her in divorce proceedings. I had immediately told her I couldn't do so as Malcolm was already my client, so I didn't hear what she was complaining about, but a large bruise under her left eye told me all I needed to know.

I stood on the other side of the cell watching him rocking back and forth. It wasn't really the image I had of a murderer. In my imagination they were tough, brutish, large men with snarling faces, a fairy tale thug, not this disturbed young man with a pale thin face and long dark curly hair who looked more like Prince Charming than a killer.

Malcolm maintained his plea of not guilty and the case was heard at Lancaster Assizes in the same court room where the Pendle witches were tried over four hundred years before. The only issue in the trial was the cause of death. Was she strangled or did she die of an overdose? The pathologist I had instructed took the view that the evidence of strangulation was weak, but when he was in the witness box, under cross examination he accused the Home Office pathologist of breaking the hyoid bone in a clumsy dissection. At that point the QC representing Malcolm came to the conclusion that a verdict of guilty was inevitable and advised him to plead guilty to manslaughter. He agreed to do so and was sentenced to serve six years in prison, some of which he served at Parkhurst in the Isle of Wight, where his brother was serving a sentence for armed robbery.

A few years later the doctor we had instructed to give evidence about the effects of taking large quantities of Methaqualone, the active ingredient of Mandrax tablets sent me a paper published in a scientific journal which argued that the level of Methaqualone, in the kidneys was a better indication of poisoning than that in the blood stream. The level in Lynn's kidney was well in excess of the safe limit described in the paper.

Battered Wives

Soon after I moved to London I was asked by the Cambridge Settlement if I would help a group of women who were trying to establish a Battered Wives Refuge in the East End of London. At that time the only safe house was the one established by the campaigner Erin Pizzey in Chiswick to the west of the capital. None of the former Cambridge graduates was a woman and the group didn't want any men coming into the house, so I was asked if I would volunteer. They had identified a suitable property, a former doctor's house and surgery on East India Dock Road. One night I found myself, a respectable member of the legal profession, (I had qualified as a solicitor three years previously) along with four other women, climbing the wall of these premises and breaking into the house through a side window. After making it habitable, getting the electricity connected and arranging to pay the rates, a number of women with their children came to live in the house.

I had been recruited, not just to sort out their illegal occupation of the house, something the GLC under Ken Livingston turned a blind eye to providing you paid the rates, but also to assist the women with their legal proceedings. In addition there were a number of social workers as some of the children were on the 'at risk' register. They also helped the families with claiming benefits etc.

The house had room for about ten women and their children. In order to ensure the place ran smoothly we established a number of rules including a cleaning rota, use of bathrooms and the kitchen etc. We decided to have a weekly meeting at which any problems could be aired and I would make appointments to see anyone who needed help with legal proceedings.

Generally things went well until this particular woman came to the house with her three children. She was very difficult, the children were always filthy and she frequently left the kitchen in a mess preferring to spend time watching television. Her husband turned up most weeks to ask if the children were alright. He seemed genuinely concerned about his family. If I was at the house I was the one who spoke to him. Unlike some of the husbands and boyfriends who came to the door, he never insisted on seeing his wife or the children. I formed the view that the woman was, to a large extent, the author of her own misfortunes. I said as much to one of the social workers who retorted that there was never an excuse for violence.

Our meetings were always held at 7.30pm on a Monday evening in the sitting room, the only shared space in the house. This particular evening, we all gathered for our meeting when this woman came in and turned on the television pronouncing that she didn't want to attend the meeting but wanted to watch East Enders. The social worker who had told me there was never any reason to assault another person, asked her to turn the TV off. When she refused, the social worker went over to the TV and switched it off. The woman got up and turned the TV back on. This was repeated a number of times with the language getting more heated until, as the woman stepped forward again towards the TV, the social worker grabbed hold of the woman by the arm, swung her round and slapped her face.

Paying the Price

Sitting in a Magistrates Court waiting for your case to come on can be very entertaining. I was doing just that at Bow Street Magistrates Court when a man was brought before the Stipendiary Magistrate for an offence of indecent behaviour in a Royal Park. The man had picked up a prostitute on Park Lane and they had gone into Hyde Park to complete the transaction. A policeman had caught them 'in delicto flagrante' under a tree.

'I allowed them time to straighten their dress which was in some disarray and then arrested them,' the officer said with the sort of straight face only a police officer in court can muster. The man pleaded guilty and the magistrate imposed a fine warning him that the consequences may be more severe if he was caught again and may result in him having to explain to his wife where he was and why.

The next person in the dock was the prostitute. She had a long list of previous offences for soliciting in a public place, but the Magistrate was reluctant to do anything other than fine her. When he told her how much she would have to pay, she asked for time.

'Have you no money with you?' the magistrate asked.

'No.'

The court officer confirmed she had only a few coins in her possession and a return ticket to Birmingham where she lived. She was one of a number of woman who came to London and solicited on Park Lane near the hotels in order to supplement their benefit.

'Did you not get paid last night?' the Magistrate said.

'No, Sir.'

'Has Mr X gone?' said the Magistrate to the court officer.

The policeman put his head round the door to the custody area, turned back and said, 'He's still here, Sir.'

'Right bring him back.'

Mr X was led back into the courtroom, somewhat bemused, and stood facing the Magistrate.

'You didn't pay her last night,' the Magistrate said, nodding towards the woman in the dock.

'No, there wasn't time.'

'Well there is now, you'll pay her fine.'

And with that both were dismissed from the Courtroom

The Man in the White Suit,

I am not referring to the journalist, Martin Bell, who stood for Parliament some years ago but to a solicitor who had an office close to West London Magistrates Court. This was before it moved to being in the shadow of the Hammersmith Flyover. I had only just started working for another local solicitor's practice as the second string advocate, when the outdoor clerk, a Welsh lady who liked a drink or two or maybe three, told me I needed to meet Bob. 'He's really good looking, and single,' she said acknowledging my own status. And so he was, six feet tall, a mop of dark hair and a sonorous voice with just a trace of an accent I recognised as being like my own. He was one of the many Lancastrians who had moved to London hoping to make their fortune in the city.

When the court doors opened in the morning, the outdoor clerk would dash across the road to see if any of our regular clients were in the cells, and to try and get our share of the unrepresented prisoners. She would then come back into the office and prepare a list of the cases we had to cover. There were two courtrooms in the building and I was meant to do the shorter list, usually with the less serious cases and the man who was the main advocate would do the more important ones. It never seemed to work out that way and I found myself covering most of the work in both courts, which brought me into contact with the 'man in the white suit.' Actually it wasn't his usual choice of dress, he normally wore a grey or navy blue pinstripe, but sometimes in the summer and when he wanted to make a dramatic entrance into court, he wore white. I liked Bob, but quickly worked out that he was not the man for me; far too volatile. However we worked well together in the courtroom even though we were competitors for business. A long list of clients meant there was too little time to see them all before the stipendiary magistrate came into court. Bob and I learnt to work the list officer so that our cases were not listed consecutively and so allowing a little time to see a client who had not yet appeared.

Defendants in the magistrates' courts are usually poor, ill educated and often have mental health problems, but many make light of their predicament and bring some humour into the proceedings. West London had its quota of drunks; homeless men who lived on and around Shepherds Bush Green. They were usually brought before the court for being drunk and disorderly, and although we wouldn't be paid both Bob and I often addressed the court on their behalf. One man, it was impossible to tell his age from his appearance he was so unkempt in a dirty mac, torn green sweater and a once white shirt, was before the court for stealing a tin of salmon. He was one of Bob's clients and this was one of his white suit days. The contrast could not have been more striking.

The defendant pleaded guilty to the theft and Bob stood up to mitigate on his behalf. He was immediately interrupted by the Magistrate, 'Your client has been in prison too many times. What am I going to do with him? Send him back for a tin of salmon?'

'That's exactly what I am asking you to do. The last time he was in custody, he got his teeth seen to. The upper jaw. He'd like to go back to get his lower ones sorted out. That's why he stole the tin of salmon. He needs a sentence of a least three months for the prison service to sort that out,' said Bob.

He got his three months. Whether he got his teeth fixed, I don't know because that winter he died of exposure, and it was me and Bob together with the list officer who organised a whip round to pay for his funeral.

Defending the Guilty

One of the most frequently asked questions of any lawyer is 'How do you defend someone you know is guilty?' The answer is it's nothing to do with me. I'm just an advocate, only a judge and jury can decide someone is guilty. Of course, it's not as simple as that. If a client tells me they are guilty, except in very particular circumstances I cannot defend them. If however they insist they are innocent, then no matter how strong the evidence is against them, the advocate's duty is to put their case to the best of their ability.

Usually, if on the basis of the evidence you have, the case looks overwhelming, any advocate would advise the client to plead guilty to the offence as doing so will probably result in him getting a less severe sentence. Sometimes that can result in the barrister or solicitor getting the sack. Very early on in my career, I learnt to be careful about the amount of pressure I put on a defendant who insisted he was innocent in the face of very convincing evidence.

The client was a juvenile and because of his age, the trial was to take place in the Juvenile Court. At that time, the prosecution, in this case, the Metropolitan Police Solicitors, was under no obligation to serve any of the witness statements. Usually, the police officer would provide a brief summary of the evidence to the lawyers involved. The charge against my client was one of arson. I was told that the fire had been very destructive but there had been no loss of life. The seat of the fire was in a community hall attached to a school and entry had been gained to the premises through the school kitchens, which joined the two buildings and were used by both. Whoever had gone into the hall had done so by way of a serving hatch and on the top edge of the glass partition was a perfect set of fingerprints. Those fingerprints were my client's. He denied he had ever been in the kitchen. He was lying and the magistrates could have deduced the reason for the lie was to cover his guilt.

He was fifteen years of age and of good character. His parents were clearly caring and supportive. Not always the case with juvenile offenders. Because of the seriousness of the fire, I believed a custodial sentence was inevitable, but if he pleaded guilty he might get a detention centre order rather than be sent to the Crown Court with the real possibility of being sentenced to Borstal training. I tried to persuade him that he should admit the offence. He refused. His parents had also tried as had my instructing solicitor. All to no avail.

I started the trial with a heavy heart, convinced I was just going through the motions until the prosecuting lawyer called the forensic expert. Usually in cases of arson the expert gives evidence as to the seat of the fire and the method by which it was started. Typically some sort of accelerant is used petrol, paraffin or alcohol. The expert told the court the fire had started in a plastic ashtray on the bar but did not give evidence of any accelerant being used.

There is a rule of thumb that one never asks a question to which you don't know the answer. I decided to take the risk.

'Is it possible the fire started as a result of somebody leaving a lighted cigarette stub in the ashtray?'

'Certainly. If someone had not stubbed out their cigarette properly, the plastic of the ashtray would melt and then ignite.'

The offence of arson require the prosecution to establish the fire was started deliberately and this they could no longer do. My client was acquitted and I was relieved my persuasion had failed.

Desperate Wives

Early in my career I did work in the family court and one afternoon I had the one of the strangest experiences. It was Friday and the court was very busy so that even after lunch the waiting hall was heaving. There were young men waiting for their cases to be called: some alone, others in groups or with teenage girls clinging to them. Dark suited solicitors, carrying large files, moved amongst the crowd, marshalling their clients, and bewigged barristers tried to take last minute instructions above the chatter and the sound of shuffling feet.

I threaded my way through the clusters of people until I found my client, Sharon Hurst, a young looking nineteen year old with long, wispy, blonde hair. There were three women with her who, I learnt, were from the Battered Wives Refuge in this coastal town. I needed to go through my instructions with Sharon so we went to look for an empty interview room, leaving the others behind in the hall.

It was one of those dark grey December days and the interview rooms looked worse than usual. I didn't like them: everyone passing from the offices and the robing room could see who was in them and although they could not hear anything, the body language was sufficient to give those passing a hint of how well, or otherwise, a conference was proceeding. This one was not going well at all. Sharon was reluctant to confirm the events described in her affidavit. I persisted, questioning her about the allegation that her boyfriend, Colin Fenton, had been waiting for her, near to the Refuge, and had followed her back there every day for the last week.

'You say here that he took your baby, Angelina, and ran off with her? You followed but couldn't keep up so you went round to the flat you shared with him?'

'Yes. I didn't know what else to do.'

'You went into the flat to get Angelina, but when you tried to leave he locked the door and you couldn't get out?'

'That's right. I hadn't any keys to the flat in my purse.'

'How did you get out?'

'He let me out.'

'Just like that?'

'Well, he'd gone on about me coming back so when I said I'd think about it, but I needed a day or two, he let me go.'

'Anything else happen whilst you were there?'

Sharon looked away, trying to find something else to focus on so that she did not have to look at me. Eventually she replied, 'What you suggesting?'

'I'm not suggesting anything, but you will be asked questions by Colin's barrister about what happened at your flat.'

There was a pause. Sharon chewed on her lower lip and then said, 'Nothing happened. Just an argument about me going back.'

I wasn't sure she was telling the truth, but I couldn't take it any further without calling her a liar, so I finished the interview by explaining we would have to wait most of the afternoon before we were called into court. Sharon went to get her three companions and they all returned to the interview room. They were anxious to give her advice and they were all smoking heavily, so I moved to one corner of the room and began to work on the brief.

As the afternoon wore on and work ceased in all but the closed family court, the place became silent. Daylight faded and, because nobody turned the light on in the room, the five of us were left waiting, in the dim light, to be called into court.

The conversation of the four women became intermittent and finally ceased. The silence was almost tangible. One of the women was about the same age as I was, certainly in her thirties. She was dressed in a style I liked, not least because it was so different from the black suits I was compelled to wear. She looked rather artistic, as if she might be a potter or something similar. Her blue coat was hip length and underneath she wore a floral-print skirt, a white scarf was twisted round her neck. Her hair was a mass of dark curls that looked like they needed combing and her face was small with large dark eyes. On the ring finger of her left hand, instead of a wedding band, she wore a ring with a large green pebble-shaped stone.

This woman began to talk in a low voice. There was an urgency in the tone that made me want to listen. 'The doctor gave me antidepressants after I had each of the kids. I had this post natal depression. You know what it's like?' She paused and looked round at the others but there was no response to her question, so she continued.

'Mind you, it wasn't really the babies that were the problem. It was him. He was always more violent just after the children were born. He'd wait 'til I was breastfeeding and then start to hit me round my head. I couldn't do nothing. Well you can't do much holding a baby in your arms, can you?'

She didn't pause for an answer but went on, 'I'd just curl up over the little'un to protect him from his dad. The other two would be crying and pulling at him to try and stop him. But it made no difference; he'd just push them away.

One year, it was the year Eddie was born, it was coming up to Christmas and I thought I've had enough. What I need is a nice quiet Christmas. So what did I do?'

She sat back, took a small, battered tin from her pocket, opened it, used the contents to prepare a thin cigarette which she lit and then inhaled deeply.

'What did I do? Christmas Eve I got my pills and crushed them into his beer. Well he was too drunk to notice. That'll keep him quiet I thought. He'll have such a headache tomorrow he won't want to get up and me and the kids can enjoy ourselves without him.'

She was tapping her left hand gently, but persistently, on the table top. 'I thought he was about to go to sleep in the chair so I got him upstairs, got his clothes off and rolled him into bed. Well, it was quiet.' she said with emphasis.

'He slept all Christmas Day and Boxing Day as well. I thought I'd killed him.'

She took a quick intake of breath, put her cupped hand to her mouth and whispered, 'Course, sometimes, I almost wish I had.'

'I kept going upstairs to see if he was still breathing. Eventually he came to. He couldn't believe he'd slept through Christmas Day and Boxing Day. He went on at me until I told him what I'd done. I got a real pasting. He threatened to go to the police about it but he didn't. For a while he laid off me, but then he started again. That's it, I thought, I'm leaving.'

The youngest shifted uneasily in her seat; she was a thin pale woman in her twenties, her long face emphasised by her shoulder length, light brown hair. Her thin white blouse partly unbuttoned, revealing a gold necklace, was tucked into the waistband of a short denim skirt. She had taken off her leather bomber jacket and hung it over the back of her chair even though it was quite chilly.

The threat to make a complaint to the police by her friend's husband must have struck a chord with the young woman because she began by saying, 'Mine did go to the police but they didn't believe him. They told him he must have fallen down drunk and that's how he'd got the cut on his head. I did laugh about it later but …..' Her voice trailed off, she looked down and took a deep breath before continuing 'Well he's a big lad; they just couldn't believe I could hit him that hard.' She turned to the older woman. 'He is a big bloke isn't he?' she asked.

'Yes. You only come up to his armpit. I'm not surprised the police didn't believe him.'

'Course he was drunk. He'd gone up town to watch Arsenal; been drinking all day leaving me with the kids. He'd promised to come home straight after the match so I could go to Bingo with my Mum. When he came in he was plastered; wanting his tea. I had a go at him and told him to make his own. He still had his silly supporter's hat on, a bowler painted in red and white stripes. He was sat there yelling about his tea, telling me what he wouldn't do to me if I didn't get him some food.'

The young woman continued 'So I picked up the poker and hit him over the head with it from behind. Once I started I just kept hitting until his hat lifted up from his head, sort of popped up, and the blood poured down his face in little streams. He looked at me, his eyes wide open; put his hands up to his face, touching it.'

She demonstrated, putting her hands to her forehead and then her cheeks. 'I think he thought that I had poured something over his head. When he looked at his hands and saw that it was blood he made a dive for me but I got out of the way and he fell onto the floor. The hat came off and there was blood everywhere.'

'I didn't know if it was the booze or me hitting him that made him fall over, but I didn't wait to find out. I grabbed the kids and ran to my mum's. I wasn't dressed properly, still had me slippers on. I didn't dare go back. So, I stayed there and the police came looking for me. They said they'd found him in the street, drunk, with this nasty cut to his head and he'd told them I'd done it. "Don't be silly." I said, "Look at me. I'm only half his size." "He's up the hospital, do you want to go and see him?" they said. "We'll take you up there if you want." "No, I think I'll wait 'til he's sobered up a bit." "Might be best." they said.'

The young woman who had been speaking put her hands to her face, covering her eyes, bent her head down towards the table, pushed her fingers through her hair, pulling it back from her face before looking round at the others and smiling tentatively at them.

'I haven't been back.' She added.

I didn't know what to think. Had both women been telling the truth? Weren't they the victims of violence not the perpetrators?

Sharon turned in her seat towards me. She appeared to be surprised that I was still there but asked when they would be going into court. I said I didn't know but the usher would call us. Sharon sighed and turned back to face her friends. The eldest of the three women reached over and patted Sharon's hand. I had hardly noticed her before but now as she tried to comfort Sharon I realised not only was she older than the others but she was dressed in more expensive clothes. Her white Mac was belted and she wore a blue silk scarf tightly knotted; both had seen better days. Her brown hair, which she wore in an untidy French pleat, was beginning to go grey and the lenses of her gold rimmed glasses were thick, emphasising her brown eyes. It was completely dark outside; the only light in the room was from the street lamps and the lighting in the corridor. A telephone began to ring somewhere in the building and there was a squeal of brakes from outside. The familiar noises, breaking the silence, acted as a stimulus and conversation was resumed. They talked about the hostel and how difficult it was living with a number of other women and children. They spoke of who let their kids run riot, who didn't do their share of cleaning the bathrooms and kitchen, who took other people's food from the fridge and who always got their own choice of television programme. The eldest of the three women made very little contribution to the discussion until the talk turned to a child who played football in the garden, kicking the ball against the wall of the house for hours on end, then she said, 'I like gardening. I miss having a garden at the hostel. It's not the same when there are lots of other people walking all over it and picking the flowers. We had a nice garden at home. I spent a lot of time out there. It got me out of the way, being in the garden, particularly when Phil was in a bad mood. I like flowers - didn't grow vegetables- perhaps a few tomatoes. Course, this time of year it's a bit bare so I'd pot up some hyacinths for the house. I'd bought a bag of them in the market. Kept some of them back for planting outside. I had a nice blue bowl; the same colour as the flowers and when they began to grow, pale green shoots coming through, I put them in it and put them on the hall table. They did look lovely.'

She paused to light a cigarette from a green and white packet and I could smell the faint scent of menthol. The older woman put the packet and a yellow cigarette lighter on the table, inhaled once and placed the cigarette on the ashtray. She continued to stare out into lamp lit street and her lower lip quivered. Was this woman about to admit to some similar incident? She began slowly and with no trace of emotion.

'He had such a temper and he came in that day in a right one. His tea wasn't strong enough; I'd folded his newspaper the wrong way. It didn't matter what I did, nothing was right.' She raised her voice slightly as if she was reliving the event. 'He was effing and blinding at me and I asked him to stop. He went from the lounge to the kitchen and back again, me following, trying to get him to stop swearing. We were pulling and pushing at each other. You know what it's like?'

The woman moved her chair back so that she was facing the rest of the group. Her voice became stronger and she spoke more emphatically. 'We were in the hall and he pulled away from me sweeping the flowers onto the floor. The pot broke, there was dirt all over the tiles and the stems of the plants were broken. I was really upset. I do like flowers. I'll give you hyacinths I thought.' She stopped and untied the scarf from around her neck, folded it neatly and put it into her pocket, pushed the sleeves of her Mac up and continued. 'So a couple of days later I asked him if he fancied a lamb stew. 'Yes' he said 'That'll be nice.' I went to the butchers and bought a bit of neckend. I made a stew with carrots and peas but instead of onions I used the hyacinth bulbs. I peeled them, chopped them and fried them just as if they were the real thing. I put them with the meat and the other vegetables in a casserole, added some beer, to disguise the taste, and cooked it. When he came in from work I gave it to him. He asked me if I was having some. I told him I'd had some earlier. He said he thought that it tasted a bit funny. ''Mine didn't'' I told him. He went on and ate it all up. After about half an hour he started to sweat and said he was going to bed; he didn't feel very well. He was in and out of bed all night going to the toilet and saying he felt sick. The next morning he looked awful; he was all grey and his eyes were dull. He told me to get the doctor. He told the doctor how bad he felt, going to the toilet all the time and feeling nauseous. The doctor said it was food poisoning and asked him what he'd eaten. He'd had a pie at lunchtime in the pub and the lamb stew. He said that the stew had tasted funny. I told the doctor mine hadn't. ''It must have been the pie.'' the doctor said. Anyway, he got a week off work. Kept on about how I'd given him a dodgy stew. I never let on, even after we separated. I've never told anyone.' She paused. 'I do like a nice garden.'

They exchanged glances but before anyone could speak the door of the family court opened, the usher appeared and Sharon's case was called on. Once in the courtroom I called Sharon to give her account of the incidents which gave rise to the application for an injunction preventing her boyfriend from contacting her. She wasn't the best of witnesses and I could see that the judge was not impressed. Then cross examination began with the boy friend's barrister asking Sharon if she wanted to stay at the Hostel or go back with Colin to her flat. Sharon hesitated.

'Of course I'd like to go back to the flat.'

The Judge interjected, 'Of course she wants to go back to her own home. That Refuge is disgusting.'

'Yes of course, your honour. But I am suggesting that the witness wants to go back to the flat with Mr Fenton.'

'Well say so.' It was clearly the end of a long day. The Judge turned to Sharon and asked her if she did want to go back to her boyfriend.

Sharon looked round the court room. First at me with a look of desperation on her face and then at Colin's barrister who was holding a piece of pale lilac notepaper in his hand. I knew what was coming. Sharon had seen the letter as well and was struggling to find an answer.

'Let me help you,' said Colin's barrister smiling, and he handed the piece of paper to the usher and asked her to give it to Sharon. Sharon looked at it. The barrister paused.

'Did you write that?'

'Yes.'

'Would you like to read it to the court?'

Sharon read out the letter she had written asking Colin to meet her at the shop near the Refuge to talk about her going back with their child, Angelina.

'You met Colin by arrangement and went back to the flat with him?'

Sharon's voice was dull 'Yes.'

'And when you were there, you had intercourse with him.'

'Yes.'

I looked at the Judge. He leant forward, 'I don't think you have any grounds for an injunction.' He turned to Sharon, 'Stop being so silly and go back home.' Then, with a swift nod, he rose and swept off the bench before anyone could get to their feet.

Once outside the courtroom, the three women wanted to know what had happened. Sharon was crying so I told them she had agreed to give Colin another chance for the sake of the child. 'That's right, isn't it?' I said. Sharon nodded her head as she wiped away the tears and blew her nose. They looked at her in amazement, turned on their heels and walked away.

Along the corridor Colin was saying goodbye to his barrister and then he walked up to Sharon and put an arm round her shoulders.

'Come on, let's go and get Angie and your things.' And, without a nod in my direction, the two of them strolled out of the building.

The usher came out of the courtroom and stood watching them for a few moments before turning to me, 'They're such liars, these people aren't they.'

'That one was.' but I wasn't sure about the others.

The Steam Roller

Stag nights can lead to young men doing very silly things. One such party had been held at St Katherine's Dock alongside Tower Bridge. As the group left they spotted a road roller parked alongside the pavement. One of their number was familiar with the mechanics of these machines and after some ribaldry, he accepted a dare to start it. He moved the vehicle a couple of yards when a police car screeched to a halt beside them. The officer asked them what was going on and one of the group tried to explain. During this conversation most of the group slipped away, leaving the driver of the road roller and two other young men. The policeman wasn't prepared to listen to any explanation and all three were arrested for taking without consent, more usually referred to as TWOC.

The three men were placed in the car and taken to Tower Bridge Police Station on the other side of the river. The road roller was potentially an exhibit so one of the officers went to retrieve it. He couldn't do so as he didn't know how to start the engine, nevermind putting it into gear. His solution was to return to the station, get the man who had moved it from the cells and get him to drive it.

Although TWOC is not the most serious offence in the calendar of crimes, because it had taken place in the square mile of the City the trial was listed at the Central Criminal Court. They were guilty of the offence although it was the most theoretical taking without consent one could imagine. Although it isn't a defence to a charge there is a principle called 'de minimis' which means if the offence is so trivial and taking into account any other issues the Crown should not proceed with a prosecution. I thought this fell into that category.

The outcome of the case was particularly important to one of the three men because he worked for the Ministry of Defence and his superiors took the view that as it was an offence of dishonesty, he would be sacked if he was convicted. Myself and counsel for the other two defendants spoke to the prosecuting barrister and tried to persuade her to drop the case but she refused. She insisted it was a serious case.

'Well it did take place outside the Tower,' one of my colleagues said.

Fortunately, the Judge was of the same view as defending counsel and suggested to the prosecution they may want to consider their position and not wasted the court's time on such a trivial matter. The prosecution decided to see sense and the case was dropped. The young men got a telling off from the Judge and they all kept their jobs.

A Date with a Judge

A few years after I had been called to the Bar, I was at a drinks party in The Temple to which a number of Judges had been invited. Amongst them was a Judge I knew quite well because he had been a solicitor and appeared at one of the London Magistrates Court on a daily basis. He was about five or six years older than me, single, quite good looking and an entertaining conversationalist so when he invited me to have dinner with him one evening I accepted. We arranged to meet the following Wednesday outside the Royal Court Theatre in Sloane Square, Chelsea.

On the day of our date, I can't remember what happened but at some time in the afternoon I realised I would be unable to get to Sloane Square by the agreed hour or at all. This was before the days of mobile phones, so I tried to ring the Court where I knew he was sitting. After some delay I was put through to the Court Clerks' room, only to be told the Judge had risen for the day and he had left the building. I tried various other numbers hoping I could catch up with him, but failed to do so.

Eventually, I was able to leave court and I went straight home. I resolved to write the Judge a short note apologising for standing him up, but didn't manage to get round to it as quickly as I should have done.

Not long after, I was instructed to represent two brothers who were facing a number of counts of burglary. They both had a number of previous convictions and were reluctant to plead guilty to these new offences, although the evidence against them was fairly conclusive. The case was listed for plea and directions, which meant they would be asked whether they were pleading guilty or not guilty.

I arrived at court determined to persuade them it was in their best interests to plead guilty to the charges on the indictment. Quite often when a defendant pleaded guilty they were sentenced immediately; this was particularly true if they were persistent offenders and the only possible outcome was a custodial sentence. I had anticipated that is what would happen with these two brothers.

When I arrived at the Court House and checked which judge would be trying the case, my heart sank when I discovered it was the Judge I had stood up the previous Wednesday. Here was a dilemma; was I to advise them to plead guilty and hope the Judge would not inflict any greater sentence because of my actions or let them plead not guilty and hopefully be in front of a different judge on a later occasion.

I decided my initial opinion was the right one, and in conference with them both I advised them to plead guilty. They were still reluctant and one of them asked me if I knew the Judge. I told them I did and that I thought he would be fair and reasonable when he passed sentence on them. I didn't reveal my indiscretion of the previous Wednesday.

They maintained their innocence and I left them in the cells and went up into court, a little relieved that I would not have to mitigate on their behalf in front of a Judge I had offended. Just as the two brothers were called into court, the dock officer called to me and said they wanted to speak to me; I had to ask the Judge to allow me a few minutes. He did so and when I spoke to my clients they said they had changed their minds and would plead guilty to the indictment.

The Judge must have felt he needed to put out of his mind my failure to keep our date, because he gave them, what I thought was a very lenient sentence.

Sisters in Crime

The Gordon sisters came from a family of travellers. One day they had arrived in High Wycombe where intending to stay over night their father had backed their caravan into a lay-by. As he did so the rear of the caravan hit a concrete lamp post. When Mr Gordon got out to inspect the damage the lamp post had cracked in two. He was killed when the arm fell and hit him on the head. With little or no education although they could all read and write, the family of mother and five sisters, lived off the proceeds of crime.

The *modus operandi,* usually abbreviated to MO, of the Gordon sisters relied on the similarity in their appearance, despite the age range from seventeen to thirty two. They were of similar height and their hair was cut to the same length, almost grazing their shoulders, and was a dark blonde with silvery highlights. They were similarly proportioned, neither too overweight nor too slim, unless they were pregnant, and they wore almost identical clothes. They all had at least one small child, and two of the children were mixed race, but they would be dressed in very similar clothing. The family acted a lot like a pack of lionesses looking after each other's children.

The sisters would go into department stores usually Marks and Spencers, in a group and then split up as they wandered around looking at clothes. Some of the items were then secreted in the back of the pushchairs. The one who had taken the clothes would then switch her pushchair with child to another of the sisters, and take that one's child.

Normally the store detectives would wait until the sister they thought they had seen taking something from the shop and hiding it at the back of their child in the pushchair was outside the store. By that time she no longer had the stolen items and would look aghast at being stopped and accused of theft. Sometimes they were caught but never all of them.

That is until CCTV.

Eventually the Gordon sisters were arrested as a result of cameras recording their activities in the shopping mall in Milton Keynes. The video showed the sisters outside Marks and Spencers transferring items of clothing from one to another. An Inspector purported to identify the sisters and accordingly they were charged with conspiracy to steal as well as a number of charges of theft against different members of the family. The trial was listed in front of Judge Slack at Aylesbury Crown Court. I was instructed to represent the eldest of the sisters, Martha.

Just before the trial was due to start an usher told me the judge wanted to see me in his chambers. In his room the Judge told me that if they all pleaded guilty he was mindful of their family responsibilities and he would not prevent them from looking after their children. I went back to the robing room and told the co-defending counsel of the Judge's indication on sentence. It took a bit of effort to persuade the girls to plead guilty to enough of the charges to satisfy the prosecution. Judge Slack did keep his promise and they were all given suspended sentences and a stiff warning about the consequences if they continued their activities.

Later the Judge told me that he wanted them to plead guilty because he knew he would not be able to avoid laughing out loud when I cross examined the officer, as he knew I would, about his ability to identify the sisters by their legs!

The sisters however did not heed his warning.

Some months later they were arrested again. This time the store detectives together with the police decided to employ different tactics. The sisters and their mother had, once again, gone to Milton Keynes to steal from the Marks and Spencer's in the shopping centre. Once they arrived on the outskirts of the city they parked their two vehicles, leaving mum to look after the cars and some of the younger children. Once inside the shopping centre they were kept under observation by a team of store detectives, who watched as they stole over twenty or so items from their favourite store. This time instead of arresting the sisters as soon as they left the shop, they were followed back to their cars, and as they unloaded the stolen items of clothing into the boot of one of them they were all arrested by police officers, including Mrs Gordon.

The case was committed for trial at Luton Crown Court on a charge of conspiracy to steal. The indictment also had a number of charges of theft and it was to those they pleaded guilty. They had no alternative. They were not so fortunate in the judge either. My recollection is that he called them a scourge on the country, a gang of modern day poachers. All of them were given custodial sentences including their mother despite her having no convictions for some years. The sentences for the sisters varied depending on their previous convictions, the youngest getting the least, but the suspended sentence imposed by Judge Slack were ordered to be served consecutively by all five.

That evening fourteen children were taken into care in the absence of anyone to look after them.

Never Call Mother

Identification issues used to be a frequent problem for the courts. The case of George Davies had highlighted how unreliable an eyewitness can be. As an aside a friend of mine, a social worker who I had met at the Battered Wives Home, was involved with the Free George Davies campaign and was one of those who dug up the cricket pitch at Headingley just before a test match.

In my case, a twenty three year old had been charged with armed robbery of a building society in the East End of London. The allegation was that he had gone into the banking hall with a sawn off shotgun, threatened the cashier to hand over the money in her till. The premises had video surveillance and the Crown were relying on the video of the scene to identify my client, who had denied being the culprit and claimed he was at home in South London at the time of the offence.

There was no other evidence. The cashier couldn't identify him, nor could any of the other customers in the office at the time. There were no fingerprints or DNA at the scene to link my client to the crime. After his arrest, he was interviewed and claimed his sister and his mother would say he was at home with them. If a suspect provides an alibi, the defence must serve a formal notice on the prosecution giving details of the alibi and the witnesses they will call to support it. The prosecution then take statements from those witnesses, in the hope of undermining them. This they had done unsuccessfully.

The video was sometimes out of focus. At other times, there was only a partial view or one that was obscured by Christmas decorations. There was one good shot of the robber's face as he turned away from the counter. He had walked towards the door and looked up directly into the camera. I played the video many times trying to decide if the man shown was my client. I wasn't sure and, of course, the jury in order to convict had to be.

The trial at the Old Bailey went well. I could see the jury were doubtful the man on the video and the defendant were the same person. I called my client to give evidence. Despite the most rigorous cross examination he maintained he had been at home on the evening of the offence. It was Christmas Eve and he had watched the television with his sister and mother. He gave an account of the programmes they had seen. His sister confirmed his story and she too was a compelling witness. I began to think I would win the case and my client would be acquitted.

Then I called the second alibi witness, his mother, and as she walked into the court I knew the case was over. Her face showed the same cheek bones, the same nose and the same eyes as the face on the video. The robber could only have been her son.

Chasing Shadows

Kings Cross in London in 1993 was well known as a place to buy or sell drugs. In order to clean up the area the police began an operation known as Operation Welwyn. Undercover officers posed as buyers and when they were offered drugs the person selling was arrested and charged with offences under The Misuse of Drugs Act 1971. They used video cameras in fixed positions and also in vans. Many people were arrested in the course of this operation and it resulted in a number of trials. There is a fine line when undercover officers make such a purchase between encouraging the crime and trapping a defendant, which is illegal, and simply taking advantage of the dealer's willingness to supply the drugs.

My client, Angela was of mixed race and in her mid-twenties. She was charged with one offence of supplying Cocaine in the form of crack. Two female police officers said they had bought cocaine from her. Angela was filmed meeting the two officers and going to a telephone booth. According to the officers they gave her two marked twenty pound notes and she then handed them the wrap containing the rocks of cocaine. That transfer of drugs and money was obscured by a large traffic sign pointing the way to Cambridge and The North. There was no question that the woman with the two officers was the defendant. She was clearly identifiable wearing a denim jacket and her long hair tied up with a brightly coloured ribbon.

Angela was arrested some time later. This was to avoid others being alerted to the ongoing operation. When she was interviewed she denied supplying drugs to the police officer but said she made a telephone call to another person who would have supplied the police woman with cocaine. If that was the truth then she would still have been guilty of the offence but on a different basis, although that difference raised the issue of entrapment. Legal argument on that point was resolved by the Crown agreeing that the jury could only return a verdict of guilty on the grounds that Angela had sold cocaine to the officers.

When the two police officers gave evidence they said they had spoken to Angela on the street and asked to buy drugs from her. She had suggested the deal took place in the telephone booth and they had followed her but had stood outside while she took the drugs out of her handbag. They had handed her two twenty pound notes in exchange for the crack. The numbers of the notes had been recorded, but none were found in Angela's possession. The Crown's explanation was she had spent it between the offence being committed and her arrest.

Although on the video recording, the traffic sign obscured not only the telephone booth but the two officers as well, I was able to follow their shadows as they crossed the pavement. At no time had they approached the telephone booth, instead after they had spoken to Angela they had walked towards a pedestrian crossing where they then became visible on the film. They were unable to explain their movements when I cross examined them.

The Judge trying the case became so interested that on his way home he drove to Kings Cross to see for himself the location of the traffic sign and the telephone booth. He summed up for an acquittal and Angela was found not guilty.

As Sober as a Judge

We like to think that our judges are, well, just, and are, at least when on the bench, upright, sober men and women. The majority are but occasionally they misbehave and the mask of respectability slips.

One day I was representing a woman, let's call her Muriel, charged with obtaining social security by fraudulently claiming benefits to which she was not entitled. As usual she was a single mum trying to support her family on too little money. I can't now remember the exact nature of the lie she had told to increase her income, but she probably failed to declare the small amount she earned from working part time. It wasn't the first time Muriel had been before the courts for similar offences although it was some years since the last conviction.

She pleaded guilty to three offences of obtaining benefit by fraud and I said what I could on her behalf. My plea in mitigation fell on deaf ears and she was sentenced to six months on each count.

My recollection is that I had other cases at court that day, so I was still in the building in the late afternoon, when I was asked to go to the cells. Once down in the bowels of the court house I was told by one of the prison officers that the judge had requested my client be taken back up to the dock. I went to see her in her cell. She was a small woman, dark eyes now red-rimmed, and dark brown hair scraped back into a pony tail. She wanted to know why the judge wanted to see her again. I told her I didn't know.

After my brief conversation with her I went back into the court room. None of the lights in the room were on; high windows let in a low grey light. The panelling around the walls, the judge's bench and all the seating were dark wood making it seem sombre and very austere. The judge's bench was raised up and stretched across the width of the room. To one side of the raised area was a red curtain hung on a heavy brass pole. Behind the curtain was the door to the judge's chambers. I was the only person in the room; there were no ushers and no clerk. After a few minutes Muriel was brought into the high dock at the rear, by two prison officers. We all waited in silence.

Suddenly the curtain was swept aside and the Judge staggered onto the bench. He was not robed save for his tabs. In his right hand he had a half full wine glass that he was waving around. He took three steps into the room turned to look at Muriel and said, 'Those sentences, they are consecutive not concurrent.' Then he raised his wineglass and said 'Cheers,' before fumbling his way back into his chambers.

The sentences being consecutive meant a term of eighteen months imprisonment not six. Fortunately the prison officers ignored the impromptu and probably illegal sentencing session and recorded the sentence as concurrent.

There must have been a fair amount of social security frauds when I was in practice as another incident with a Judge behaving badly also concerned a woman who had obtained welfare payments by deception. My own opinion was that too many Judges had no idea how difficult it was to manage on so little money. Most lawyers would have thought nothing about paying forty pounds for a pair of children's shoes – it was less than they would spend on a bottle of wine. But the law is the law and it is taxpayers money.

I was instructed to represent a young woman charged with the offence of obtaining welfare payments by deception. It wasn't her first court appearance and she had been given a suspended prison sentence to enable her to see a psychologist in the hope that dealing with some of her many problems would stop her reoffending. It had not and although the Probation Officer was asking for another chance – she had failed to keep all the appointments with the psychologist, on occasions for perfectly proper reasons – I thought she was likely to go to prison. No one should forget that sending a woman to prison often means that children have to go into care.

Despite my own opinion I stood up to mitigate and ask the Judge to consider taking the course that the Probation Officer suggested, which I think was another period on Probation. The Judge was not having it and kept interrupting me. I persisted in mitigating on behalf of my client in accordance with my instructions. At which point the Judge lost it and began to yell at me that I was to cease immediately. 'With respect Your Honour,' a respect I was not feeling at that precise moment, 'If I can just finish...'

'No you cannot,' he said.

'But, Your Honour...' I was interrupted again.

'Sit down. Sit down.' By this time the Judge was purple in the face and looked like he was bursting at the seams. I expected his wig to begin bouncing on his head.

At first I didn't sit down, because I thought he would see he was being unreasonable and hear me out and then impose whatever custodial sentence he thought appropriate. Instead he began to roar at me to sit down. This time I complied. He stormed off the Bench, leaving me in the courtroom. The ushers, clerk, prison staff and warrant officer were all open mouthed at his behaviour.

He sent a message that the case was to be transferred to another court where the Judge who had imposed the suspended sentence was sitting and he did treat her with some leniency and made the Probation Order.

That episode with such a difficult judge contributed, I believe, to the decision by the Lord Chancellor's Office to refuse my application for Silk. It wasn't the events in Court but my reaction to it, which meant I was thought to be 'not quite the right style for Silk.'

The Judge's behaviour towards me in the course of that hearing had left me feeling rather bruised. In my view I had been belittled in Court in front of my client, other barristers, solicitors and probation staff. Many of the Court staff were shocked by his behaviour and had apologised as if it was their fault.

I heard nothing from the Judge until a couple of weeks later I was at the same court and one of the court clerks said the Judge would like to see me in Chambers. I asked if prosecuting counsel in my case was wanted as well.

'No. He's just asked for you. I think it is about the other week.'

We both knew what she meant. I didn't want to go and see him at 10am before Court sat, not least because he liked to offer a glass of sherry to counsel invited to his chambers. It was far too early for me to drink alcohol, but the Judge could be very persistent and it was difficult to refuse. On other occasions I had poured mine into the soil surrounding a potted plant, but on my own I would find that impossible. But, and more importantly to me, his rude remarks had taken place in open court, I felt he should make his apology in court as well. I knew it was never going to happen.

I declined his invitation and although there was never a repetition of that scene, nevertheless I had clearly been struck off his Christmas Card list (not that I was ever on it) and I suspect was deemed by him to be unsuitable for Silk.

The following pages are the first chapter of my novel 'Crucial Evidence.' The case described and the characters are entirely fictional although the law and the emotions and behaviour of the protagonist Cassie Hardman are based on my experiences.

Crucial Evidence

Chapter 1

Cassie opened the brown covered album of photographs, marked Exhibit 1, and found herself looking at the face of a young woman; the blonde hair had been pulled back from the forehead, the eyelids closed, long lashes curled on the high cheekbones, the skin was pale but the lips still bore a trace of raspberry pink lipstick. There was no hint of the violence that had ended the woman's life. Cassie studied the face, compelling in its calm beauty. She traced the outline of the lips with her finger; she felt a sense of loss at this life cut short, then she turned the pages to the photographs of the woman's body, which revealed how she had met her death. Blood from a single stab wound below her left breast had dried into strange shapes across the skin of her torso, defiling her model girl figure. Cassie closed the album quickly; she had seen enough.

She picked up another set of pictures; these showed the scene of the murder, taken some weeks later, in daylight, and after the leaves had fallen from the trees. Holland Walk looked like a country lane, tree-lined on one side and a high brick wall on the other, rather than a pedestrian thoroughfare in the middle of London. Cassie knew Holland Park was closed after dark, but the Walk was not; she had taken that way home often since she had moved to her flat in Notting Hill, but never alone. The path was poorly lit, the overhanging trees created areas of deep shade; just the sort of place for a murder.

She pushed the photograph albums back across the large oak desk, made for her by her grandfather, and because of that, her most treasured possession, and leant back pushing her hands through her short brown hair. The light had faded, and from the windows of her flat, on the top floor of a white-stuccoed house, she let her eyes follow the lights of aircraft heading towards Heathrow, winking across the night sky, then she stood up and leant across the desk to close the curtains, before heading for the kitchen to make her evening meal.

She liked cooking; she had no time for hobbies, but she had to eat, and rather than snack she cooked herself a meal most evenings. Her mother had worked at a bakery until Cassie was born, and while she stayed at home to look after her children - Cassie had a younger sister Amanda - she had started making cakes for birthdays and weddings to supplement the family income. Cassie had spent her early years in her mother's kitchen, standing on a stool, helping to stir the treacle into gingerbread mixes and the dried fruit into cake batter. Her mother was convinced Cassie would become a chef, and had been shocked at a parent's evening, when in response to her comment that she hoped Cassie would go to the Catering College in Blackpool, the headmistress had said she hoped for better things for Cassie. That hope, kindled seventeen years ago, had given life to her ambition, taking her from Lancaster to 3 Burke Court, a set of barristers' Chambers in the Temple.

She continued to cook, experimenting with different recipes, making simple but tasty dishes to enjoy with a glass of wine. It had become her way of winding down and doing something creative for a short while; an interlude between finishing in court and the preparation for the next day, or the next trial. Now she wilted some young spinach with salt, pepper and nutmeg, seared a piece of salmon and ate it slowly, with bread from a local French Bakery, and a glass of Chablis. When she had finished she went back to her desk and turned on the reading lamp, before picking up one of the two black lever-arch files, containing the trial papers.

The name of the dead woman was Shelley Paulson. Her mother, who had identified the body, believed her daughter was a director of a successful employment agency providing PAs for overseas businessmen. The reality was she worked as an escort, accompanying lone men to dinner and providing more intimate services for which she had been well paid. She had been able to buy and furnish a luxurious flat in one of the garden squares in Notting Hill. Amongst the items taken by the police from her home were the paraphernalia of a drug user, a broken mirror, squares of aluminium foil and a few small packets of a white powder; something else of which her mother was unaware. Cassie tried to imagine what Mrs Paulson might have felt; the shock when the policemen came to the door, the nightmare of the journey to the mortuary, hoping they were wrong and it wasn't her child, and then, looking at the beautiful face, realizing it was true, and in that single moment the axis of her world shifting.

How Shelley had died was not the issue for Cassie, it was who was responsible. Her client, Lenny Barker, had been charged with the murder and he was pleading not guilty; she had to prepare his defence. She was meeting him the next day to discuss the evidence, and even though she wouldn't be the one to decide what questions to ask the witnesses, or be making a speech to the jury, some senior barrister, probably a silk, someone with the magic initials QC behind his name, would be doing that, never the less she needed to have all the facts at her fingertips. She wanted to impress with her understanding of the case and the issue of identification on which the trial would turn.Cassie moved on to the second file which contained the witness statements, reports and police logs that were thought unnecessary for the prosecution case. Although none of them would be used in the course of the trial, sometimes they provided information that would assist the defence, or give the lawyers a better understanding of the police investigation. She flicked through them, in case there was anything she needed to ask Barker about. Most of them were the evidence of friends and clients of the dead woman's, but then she found a report from a fingerprint expert who had compared prints taken from a silver bracelet worn by Shelley Paulson at the time of her death, and the fingerprints taken from Lenny Barker on his arrest. The expert had come to the conclusion that there were insufficient ridge characteristics for her to say, with any certainty, that any of the fingerprints on the bracelet were made by Barker. Cassie picked up the copy prints, held them close to the light, and examined them carefully. The first sheets showed clear prints of all eight of Lenny Barker's fingertips and both thumbs; they were clear, the lines well defined. The print from the middle finger had six tiny paper arrows pointing to ridges and whorls, the identifying marks of the print. On the sheet which showed the prints found on the bracelet a number of prints were smudged where the hand making them had dragged across the surface of the exhibit, and others were overlaid as if one hand had been placed where another had already been. That too had arrows pointing to significant marks. She compared them and, although she was not the expert, came to the conclusion they were probably identical. Certainly she would not want a jury to see them; she felt sure they, like her, would come to the conclusion the prints on the bracelet were Barkers, despite the expert's report

    She closed the file and tied the papers together before putting them in her holdall, and then went to the kitchen to clear up after her evening meal. The sense of wellbeing she had been given by the food and wine had vanished, dispelled by the discovery of the fingerprint report. Now the conference would be a formality; Lenny Barker was just another defendant trying to escape responsibility for his crime.

Reviews of Crucial Evidence.

Author Margaret Barnes spent twenty-five years in England's court system. Her mastery of understanding that system shows in Crucial Evidence. Barnes delineates the details of Lenny Barker's case. Lenny is charged with the brutal murder of prostitute Shelley Paulson. His defense barrister is Cassie Hardman. At first Cassie is sure Lenny is the killer though she's astute in recognizing a latent charm that could be innocence. When she uncovers new evidence during her investigation she risks her career to pursue an elusive killer.

The author draws on her experience in the practice of law to create a realistically vivid portrayal of London's legal system. The intricate detail of the various actors and roles provides a necessary solid (factual) foundation for the fictional account with the real-time, verbatim court proceedings stations the reader in the gallery of this tensely mesmerising drama.

A thoroughly good read with good pace and absorbing detail. The action centres on two feisty and principled female characters. Through Cassie, Lenny's defence lawyer, we gain insights into the political manoeuvrings which bedevil career advancement in legal chambers. The experiences of both Cassie and her police counterpart, Alex, highlight the latent misogyny which still occasionally surfaces in many walks of life. The descriptions of the Holland Park area of London are navigated with skill and all the characters, whether market traders, Lenny and his family, or legal colleagues are convincingly portrayed.

Debut novel by this author drawing on her own experiences at the English Bar; an intriguing courtroom drama with some interesting characters. Cassie a determined young barrister is instructed by her Chambers to defend a young man who has been arrested for the murder of a young woman who had worked as an escort. A very believable and compulsive account of the trial and an insight into the inner workings at The Old Bailey in the pursuit of Justice. Certainly an author to keep an eye on.

The author Margaret Barnes was born in Lancashire and went to University in Sheffield where she obtained a law degree. She qualified as a solicitor in 1971 after doing articles with a firm in Blackpool, Lancashire. She moved to London in 1973 and then decided she really wanted to address a jury. She was called to the Bar in 1976 and retired after twenty five years defending the indefensible.

She describes herself a Lancastrian Londoner but lives in exile in Devon with her husband and their Springer Spaniel

Cover design by BerniStevensdesign.com

Printed in Great Britain
by Amazon